Nicola Brown

More about Bonzo

Ernst Klett Schulbuchverlag
Stuttgart Düsseldorf Berlin Leipzig

Contents

Gedruckt auf Recyclingpapier,
hergestellt aus 100% Altpapier.

1. Auflage 1 13 12 | 2004

Dieses Werk folgt im Deutschen der reformierten Rechtschreibung und Zeichensetzung.
Alle Drucke dieser Auflage können im Unterricht nebeneinander benutzt werden, sie sind untereinander unverändert.
Die letzte Zahl bezeichnet das Jahr dieses Druckes.

Internetadresse: http://www.klett-verlag.de
Zeichnungen zu Umschlag und Text: Christine Georg.
Satz: Lihs, Satz und Repro, Ludwigsburg.
Druck: Druckhaus Vogel GmbH, 70771 L.-Echterdingen.
Printed in Germany.
ISBN 3-12-571240-8

Introduction

"More about Bonzo" is a collection of four short plays written in easy English and centred around a great favourite of many German pupils, the loveable dog Bonzo. Vocabulary and structures are based on *Red line 1, Green Line 1* and *Orange Line 1,* but any class which has been learning English for about a year can have fun acting out these plays.
The playlets vary in length and in the size of their cast. But most of the roles are very short, so there are no long passages to be memorized. And in the last play "Bonzo goes on a picnic" there are enough roles for everyone in the class to be able to join in. Bonzo is probably the most difficult part to play, as it is important that the humorous side of his character is really brought alive. At times he must take on the role of the narrator, introducing and commenting on the action, and at other times he becomes involved in the scene himself. It is important to remember that Bonzo never speaks directly to the other characters. He just verbalizes his thoughts for the audience.
The plays can be tackled in a number of different ways. They can simply be read in class, or they can be recorded on cassette or on video and played back. This then gives the pupils the opportunity to assess their own performances. The plays are, however, really designed to be acted out. With a limited number of props the scenes can really come to life. The beach scene, for example, can be portrayed with towels, buckets and spades and a picnic basket.
Once the plays have been rehearsed in class, there's no reason why they can't be performed in front of an audience, at a parent teacher meeting, at a school fete or a similar event. So good luck with the plays.

Bonzo and the burglar

Characters

Bonzo
Mrs Wilson
Mandy Wilson
Peter Wilson
Mr Wilson
Burglar
Policewoman
Policeman

Scene 1

In the Wilsons' sitting-room. Peter is watching TV, Mandy is reading a book and Bonzo is sitting on his chair. He is watching the children and is thinking.

Bonzo *(thinks)* It's Saturday morning. Mr and Mrs Wilson and Mandy and Peter are going shopping. Mandy and Peter aren't very happy. They don't like shopping. Especially when they have to buy their

burglar ['bɜ:glə] Einbrecher(in)
character ['kærəktə] Charakter, Person
policeman/-woman [pə'li:swʊmən] Polizist(in)
to go shopping ['ʃɒpɪŋ] einkaufen gehen
especially [ɪ'speʃəlɪ] besonders
to have to müssen

school uniforms. But then I'm not very happy either. It's a very sunny day today. Great for a picnic or for a walk with my people. But they don't even want to take me to the shops with them. And I love cars. Sometimes my people can be very difficult.

Mrs Wilson *(She comes into the room.)* Mandy, Peter, come on. We are going shopping now. Dad and I are waiting for you.
Mandy Oh no! I want to read my book. "Tom, the boy who eats chairs". It's so good.
Peter And I want to watch "Superman". It's really great. Then I want to watch ...
Mrs Wilson Well, you can't.
Mandy Please can we stay here, Mum?
Mr Wilson No, you can't. I don't want to go shopping either. But we have to buy *your* school uniforms.
Peter Oh no! Not again.
Mrs Wilson Yes, again! Mandy needs a new skirt and you need some trousers and a blazer. Come on. Let's go.

not ... either ['aɪðə] auch ... nicht
to love [lʌv] lieben
to need [ni:d] brauchen

Peter Can we take Bonzo?
(Bonzo looks at Mr and Mrs Wilson.)

Mr and Mrs Wilson No.

Mrs Wilson Bonzo must stay here.

Mandy But he likes to go out in the car.

Mrs Wilson But Bonzo doesn't like to wait outside shops. And shop assistants don't like lots of Bonzos in their shops. He can stay here.

Mr Wilson He can look after the house like other dogs. Okay? Can we go now?

Scene 2

Later that morning. The Wilsons arrive home. They get out of the car.

Mr Wilson I'm so tired.

Mandy and Mrs Wilson Me, too.

Peter Me three!
(They all laugh.)

Peter Can you open the door? I want to watch TV. Perhaps I can see my programme.

Mrs Wilson No. You can carry some of the shopping first. Here is your blazer and here are your trousers.

tired [ˈtaɪəd] müde
programme [ˈprəʊgræm] Sendung

Mr Wilson	And you watch too much television. It's bad for you.
Mandy	Why?
Mr Wilson	You get square eyes.
Mandy	Really?
Peter	No, silly!
Mandy:	Square eyes. Square eyes.
Mrs Wilson	Sssssh.
Mr Wilson	What's the matter?
Mandy	What?
Mr Wilson	The dining-room window is broken. Look.
Mrs Wilson	Oh dear! Perhaps we've got burglars.
Peter and Mandy	Burglars!
Mrs Wilson	Mandy and Peter, go and sit in the car. Don't say a word. Go on. *(Mandy and Peter get in the car.)* But I don't understand. Where is Bonzo?
Mr Wilson	Good question. Where *is* he? Perhaps he's sleeping on Peter's bed. Oh, Bonzo. It's his job to look after the house. What can we do? Perhaps the burglars are dangerous.

to get bekommen
square [skweə] viereckig
broken [ˈbrəʊkən] gebrochen
dangerous [ˈdeɪndʒərəs] gefährlich

Mrs Wilson	Perhaps they aren't there now. It's very quiet. Let's open the front door. But we mustn't make a noise. Here's the key. *(Mr and Mrs Wilson go to the front door. Peter and Mandy watch from the car. They are afraid.)*

Scene 3

Inside the house

Mrs Wilson	*(She is whispering.)* I can't hear a thing. It's really quiet.
Mr Wilson	Where's Bonzo? *(He whispers Bonzo's name.)* Bonzo, Bonzo.
Mrs Wilson	*(She goes into the sitting-room.)* Ssh. Look. We *have* got burglars. Our picture isn't on the wall.
Mr Wilson	But our TV is still there.
Mrs Wilson	But our record-player isn't there. Oh dear. Do you think they're still here?
Mr Wilson	I don't know. Give me your umbrella. *(Mrs Wilson gives him her umbrella.)*
Mrs Wilson	What are you doing?

quiet ['kwaɪət] leise
to whisper ['wɪspə] flüstern
not a thing [θɪŋ] überhaupt nichts
record-player ['rekɔ:d ˌpleɪə] Plattenspieler
umbrella [ʌm'brelə] Regenschirm

Mr Wilson	I don't really know. I can hit the burglar with it.
Mrs Wilson	Wait a minute. Can you hear Bonzo? He's barking.
Mr Wilson	Yes I think so. Where is he?
Mrs Wilson	I think he's in the garden.
Mr Wilson	Why doesn't he come in? He always comes and says hello. Let's look for him. *(Mr and Mrs Wilson go into the kitchen.)*
Mrs Wilson	I can see him. Bonzo *is* in the garden. Oh dear. He's got the burglar's leg in his mouth.
Mr Wilson	I can see our record-player. It's on the grass. And our picture. Quick. Let's go back into the dining-room. The burglar mustn't see us.

to hit [hɪt] schlagen, *mouth* [maʊθ] Mund, *hier* Schnauze

Mrs Wilson	Good idea! We can telephone the police from there.
	(They go into the dining-room. Mrs Wilson calls the police.)
Policewoman	Hello. Fulford Police Station.
Mrs Wilson	Hello. It's Mrs Wilson from 6 Fordlands Road. There's a burglar in our garden. Our dog is holding him there. Can you come now?
Policewoman	Yes, of course. Just give us two minutes.

Scene 4

In the Wilsons' sitting-room. A policeman and a policewoman are standing next to the burglar. The burglar is wearing handcuffs. He is looking very unhappy.

Peter	Well done, Bonzo! Isn't he a clever dog?
Policeman	Yes. He really is very clever.
Policewoman	We need dogs like Bonzo. Do you want a job, Bonzo?
	(Bonzo looks at the floor.)
Bonzo	*(thinks)* Me, a police dog. Oh no!

Fulford [ˈfʊlfəd]
Fordlands [ˈfɔːdlənz]
handcuffs [ˈhændkʌfs] Handschellen
Well done! [ˌwelˈdʌn] Gut gemacht!

Mandy	He doesn't think it's a very good idea. I think it's a silly idea, too. He's *our* dog.
Policeman	*(He laughs.)* It's okay. You can keep Bonzo.
Peter	Some more biscuits, Bonzo?
Bonzo	Woof.
Mandy	He's the cleverest dog in York.
Peter	No, he's not, silly. He's the cleverest dog in England. Do you want another biscuit, Bonzo?

to keep [ki:p] behalten
the cleverest dog ['klevərɪst] der klügste Hund

Bonzo Woof, woof.
(thinks) Sometimes my people can be clever, too.

1. *Why do Peter and Mandy want to stay at home?*
2. *Why must they go to the shops with their mother and father?*
3. *Why can't Bonzo go with them?*
4. *How do Mr and Mrs Wilson know they've got burglars?*
5. *What is Bonzo doing in the garden?*
6. *What does Bonzo think of the policewoman's idea? (What do you think of the idea?)*

Bonzo's Christmas

Characters

Bonzo
Mr Wilson
Mrs Wilson
Mandy Wilson
Peter Wilson
Shop-assistants
Shoppers
Policewoman

Scene 1

At home on the morning of December 24th. Mandy and Peter are writing some Christmas cards. Mr Wilson is cleaning the kitchen floor. Mrs Wilson is writing a shopping list. Bonzo is watching TV. Christmas music is playing.

Christmas ['krɪsməs] Weihnachten
character ['kærəktə] Charakter, Person
shopper ['ʃɒpə] Kunde/-in
policewoman [pə'lɪswʊmən] Polizistin
shopping list ['ʃɒpɪŋ ˌlɪst] Einkaufsliste

Bonzo *(thinks)* Oh dear. It's that silly time of the year again. Christmas. Every year it's the same. Mr and Mrs Wilson, Mandy and Peter buy their presents on the last day. On December 24th. The shops are all full. Everyone is angry. They come home from the shops and are tired and angry, too. Then on Christmas Day they are very tired. So they sleep all afternoon. Why are people so silly? But there's one nice thing about Christmas – I get a nice Christmas dinner.

the same [seɪm] das Gleiche
present ['prezənt] Geschenk
tired ['taɪəd] müde

Mr Wilson Well, the floor is clean. I must go to the shops now.

Mrs Wilson I want to go to the shops, too.

Mandy and Peter Me, too.

Mr Wilson Oh!
Mrs Wilson Oh dear!
Mandy Oh!
Peter Oh dear! *(Together)*

Mrs Wilson I just need a few things.
Mr Wilson I only want to get one present.
Mandy I need something for Grandma. *(Together)*

Peter And I haven't got a present for Bonzo.

Bonzo *(thinks)* That's a good idea. Let me think. What do I want? ... A box of chocolates, some big sausages and a nice raincoat like Fred the cat next door.

Mrs Wilson Do you need the car?

Mr Wilson Well, I can go by bus. What about you, Peter?

Peter I can take my bike.

Mandy Can I come with you, Mum?

Mrs Wilson Well, I only want to go in one shop. In Greens. It's probably very difficult to park today. Where do you want to go?

to need [ni:d] brauchen
Grandma ['grænmɑ:] Oma
sausage ['sɒsɪdʒ] Wurst
probably ['prɒbəblɪ] wahrscheinlich
to park [pɑ:k] parken

Mandy I want to go to Greens, too. I need a present for Grandma.

Mrs Wilson Okay. Then you can come with me. But I can't wait for you.

Peter Bonzo, where are you going?

(Bonzo goes to the door.)

Mandy He wants to go shopping, too.

Mrs Wilson He doesn't want to go shopping. He wants to go out in the car. No, Bonzo. You can stay here.

(Bonzo looks very unhappy.)

Mandy Oh can't he come, Mum? It *is* Christmas.

Mrs Wilson Oh, okay then. Because it's Christmas. But don't bark at the other dogs, Bonzo. Be nice to them. It's Christmas, you know.

(Mrs Wilson, Mr Wilson, Bonzo, Peter and Mandy leave the house together. Mandy, Bonzo and Mrs Wilson get in the car. Mr Wilson walks to the bus stop. Peter gets on his bike.)

Mandy Bye, Dad, Bye, Peter.

Mr Wilson Bye.

Mrs Wilson Bye, darling.

Mr Wilson Bye. See you later.

to go shopping ['ʃɒpɪŋ] einkaufen gehen
darling ['dɑ:lɪŋ] Liebling
See you later. Bis später.

Scene 2

Mrs Wilson parks the car in front of Greens. Mandy and Mrs Wilson get out of the car.

Mrs Wilson	Oh dear. The town is so full. I can't really park here.
Mandy	Is it illegal?
Mrs Wilson	Yes. Never mind. We must be very quick.
Mandy	What about Bonzo?
Mrs Wilson	He must stay in the car.
Bonzo	*(thinks)* Why must I stay in the car? There's a silly cat over there. I want to run after it.
Mandy	But he doesn't want to. Perhaps he wants to buy some Christmas presents.
Mrs Wilson	Mandy! Don't be silly. Bonzo must wait in the car. Let's meet at the cash desk in Greens in 15 minutes. Okay?
Mandy	Okay. Bye-bye, Bonzo.

illegal [ɪˈliːgl] illegal
quick [kwɪk] schnell
cash desk [ˈkæʃ ˌdesk] Kasse

Scene 3

Fifteen minutes later. At the cash desk. Some shoppers are looking at the clothes and others are waiting at the cash desk. The shop-assistants are answering the shoppers' questions.

Mrs Wilson	It's terrible in here. It's so full.
Mandy	I'm really hot.
Mrs Wilson	Have you got your present for Grandma?
Mandy	Yes. I've got some chocolates.
Mrs Wilson	I just need one more thing.
Mandy	What?
Mrs Wilson	A Christmas pudding.
Mandy	Mum, Mum. I can hear Bonzo. He's barking.
Mrs Wilson	He's just barking at the other dogs again.
Mandy	No, he's not. He's telling us something.
Mrs Wilson	Don't be silly, Mandy. He often barks at the other dogs.
Mandy	Yes, I know. But this time he's trying to tell us something. Come on. *(Mandy runs out of the shop. Mrs Wilson runs after her.)*
Mandy	Look, Mum.
Mrs Wilson	What's the matter?

Christmas pudding [ˈkrɪsməs ˌpʊdɪŋ] Plumpudding
to try [traɪ] versuchen

Mandy On the other side of the road.

Mrs Wilson Oh there's a policewoman. It's our lucky day. Good boy, Bonzo. Aren't you clever? Come on, Mandy. Let's go home.

Scene 4

In the Wilsons' sitting-room. Peter and Mr Wilson are already at home when Mandy, Mrs Wilson and Bonzo come in.

Mandy Good old Bonzo. Aren't you a clever dog? You can have a special Christmas dinner tomorrow.

Mrs Wilson Christmas dinner. Oh no!

Peter What's the matter, Mum?

Mrs Wilson It's the Christmas dinner.

Peter What?

Mrs Wilson We haven't got a Christmas pudding this year and Greens is shut now.

Peter No Christmas pudding? Why not? *(Bonzo barks. Mandy laughs.)*

Mandy Bonzo and I know why. It's our little secret.
(Bonzo goes and sits in his chair and looks happy.)

side [saɪd] Seite
already [ɔːlˈredɪ] schon

1. *What usually happens in the Wilson family on December 24th and 25th?*
2. *Why mustn't Bonzo bark at the other dogs?*
3. *Where does Mrs Wilson park?*
4. *Why does Bonzo bark when they are in the shop?*
5. *Why is Bonzo happy?*
6. *What do you usually do on December 24th? And on December 25th?*

Bonzo and the Smiths

Characters

Bonzo
Mr Wilson
Mandy Wilson
Peter Wilson
Mrs Wilson
Mrs Smith
Mr Smith
Caroline Smith
Nigel Smith
Fritz

Scene 1

In the dining-room. Mr and Mrs Wilson are sitting at the table. They are eating their breakfast.

Mr Wilson	Mandy, Peter. Breakfast. Come on. It's 9 o'clock. What are you doing?
Mandy	*(shouts from her bedroom)* I'm reading my comic.
Mr Wilson	Well, come downstairs. It's time for breakfast. The Smiths are coming today. Peter, what are you doing?
Peter	*(shouts from his bedroom)* I'm sleeping.

character [ˈkærəktə] Charakter

Mrs Wilson No, you're not. Come downstairs. It's time for breakfast. There's eggs and toast and cornflakes and ...

Peter So what? I'm not hungry.

(Mandy comes into the dining-room with her comic in her hand.)

Mr Wilson Oh, Mandy! What are you wearing?

Mandy My jeans.

Mr Wilson Yes, I can see that. But the Smiths are coming today. Can't you put on something nice?

(Peter comes into the room.)

Mandy Oh no! Not *them*.

Mrs Wilson Mandy!

Peter Oh no! Why are they coming again?

Mrs Wilson They're staying with us for the weekend. Then they are going to Scotland for a holiday. Peter, please put on some nice clothes, too.

Peter But I *am* wearing something nice. My old jeans and my Superman shirt. I'm the only boy in my class with a Superman shirt!

Mrs Wilson Peter! Put on some other trousers. Just for today.

So what? Na und?
something nice ['sʌmθɪŋ] etwas Nettes
weekend [ˌwi:k'end] Wochenende

Peter	When do they arrive?
Mrs Wilson	At about 11. But we must clean the house first. You must both clean your bedrooms.
Mandy	Why?
Mr Wilson	Because your bedrooms are both very dirty and very untidy. Nigel is sleeping in Peter's room and Caroline in Mandy's room.
Mandy	Caroline, in *my* room. But she's so silly.
Peter	And Nigel is so boring. He talks about computers all the time.
Mr Wilson	Look, they're only coming for one weekend. And they've got a dog now. You can all play together with Bonzo and their dog.
Peter	What dog have they got?
Mrs Wilson	A poodle, I think.
	(Bonzo goes and sits on a chair. He isn't very happy.)
Mandy	A poodle. I don't like poodles. They're silly dogs.
Peter	Yes. Only funny people have poodles.
Mr Wilson	You're terrible today. Here, eat your breakfast.
Peter	I'm not hungry now.
Mrs Wilson	Then go and clean your rooms!
	(Peter and Mandy leave the room.)

untidy [ʌn'taɪdɪ] unordentlich
boring ['bɔ:rɪŋ] langweilig
poodle ['pu:dl] Pudel

Bonzo	*(thinks)* Oh no! The Smiths are coming. Those funny people. And now they've got a funny dog. Poor me! I don't want to play with a poodle. Oh help! Perhaps I can hide under Peter's bed. Or I can say I'm ill. Then I can sleep on Peter's bed all day.

Scene 2

Later that morning. The doorbell rings. It is the Smiths.

Mrs Wilson	*(She opens the door.)* Hello, Sally. Hi, Tom. Nice to see you again.
Mrs Smith	Hello, Mary.
Mr Wilson	Hello. Can I take your bags?
Mr Smith	Oh, thanks a lot. Nigel, Caroline, you remember Peter and Mandy?
Caroline	Yes, of course.
Peter and Mandy	Hello.
Mrs Smith	We've got a new dog. This is Fritz. He's really sweet. Do you like him, Mandy?
Mandy	Oh ... eh ... yes!
Mrs Smith	Perhaps Bonzo and Fritz can play together.

to hide [haɪd] sich verstecken
to ring [rɪŋ] läuten

Peter	Bonzo doesn't like poodles. He usually runs after them in the park.
Mr Smith	Oh dear. We don't want that.... You're a big boy now, Peter. How old are you?
Peter	Eleven.
Mrs Smith	Eleven already? Nigel is still ten. Perhaps you can play together. Nigel has his toy cars with him. And he really likes computers.
Peter	Yes, I remember.
Mr Wilson	Perhaps the children can all go for a walk together later. They can take the dogs with them.
Nigel	Fritz can't walk very far. He gets tired.
Peter	Bonzo doesn't get tired. He can walk for miles.
Mr Wilson	Who wants a drink before lunch?
Mrs Smith	Oh, yes please. That's a good idea.

Scene 3

At lunch

Nigel	Mum, I don't like sausages.
Mrs Smith	No, he doesn't. Oh dear. Well, just leave them on your plate, Nigel.

to get tired [ˈtaɪəd] müde werden
sausage [ˈsɒsɪdʒ] Wurst
plate [pleɪt] Teller

Mandy Bonzo can eat them. He really likes sausages.
(Bonzo goes to Nigel. He puts his paw on Nigel's leg.)

Mr Smith Oh no! Not at the table. We don't like that. Dogs are dirty, you know.

Mr Wilson He doesn't usually do that. Perhaps he's hungry.

Mrs Wilson No, he's got his dinner. I just gave it to him.
(Peter leaves the room and goes into the kitchen.)

Peter Oh no! Fritz is eating Bonzo's dinner.

Mandy What! Oh, that's not fair. Poor Bonzo.

Mrs Wilson Never mind. Put Nigel's sausages on Bonzo's plate. Then everyone is happy.
(Mandy takes the plate into the kitchen. Bonzo goes into the kitchen after her.)

Mr Wilson So, who wants some ice-cream?

Caroline and Nigel Ooh, yes please.

Mr Smith Me, too.

Mrs Smith What's that noise?

paw [pɔ:] Pfote
I just gave it to him. [geɪv] Ich habe es ihm gerade gegeben.
fair [feə] gerecht
ice-cream [ˌaɪsˈkri:m] Eiskrem

Mr Wilson	It's the dogs again. They're fighting. *(They all run into the kitchen.)*
Peter	Bonzo is hiding under the table.

Mandy	Poor Bonzo. What's the matter?
Peter	Look, Fritz is eating Bonzo's last sausage. Your dog is terrible, Nigel.
Nigel	No, he's not. Fritz is just afraid of Bonzo.
Mandy	I think Bonzo is afraid of your silly poodle.
Mrs Wilson	Come on, children. Calm down. Why don't you all go for a walk? Take a ball with you. It's a really nice day.
Nigel	I want to read my computer book.

to fight [faɪt] kämpfen
to calm down [ˌkɑːm ˈdaʊn] sich beruhigen

Mr Smith	You can take it with you, Nigel. But I think a walk is a super idea. It's such a nice sunny day today.
Mrs Smith	Nigel and Caroline are such clever children. Caroline is first in her class. And Nigel is good with computers. It's his hobby.
Peter	*(to Mandy)* His hobby! That's a funny hobby. *(Mandy laughs.)*

Scene 4

That evening. Peter, Mandy, Nigel and Caroline come home after the walk. Caroline is carrying Fritz.

Mrs Wilson	How are you? Good afternoon?
Caroline	I'm very tired. It's so far to the park. Poor Fritz is very tired, too.
Nigel	I'm going to Peter's room. I want to read my computer book.
Caroline	Yes, I want to read my biology book, too. *(They leave the room.)*
Peter	They're so boring. They don't like games and they don't like parks …
Mandy	And they don't like Bonzo. And they have a silly dog …
Mr Wilson	Ssh. Perhaps the others can hear you.
Peter	Where are Mr and Mrs Smith?

biology [baɪˈɒlədʒɪ] Biologie

Mr Wilson	They're upstairs, too.
Mrs Wilson	Never mind. They're only here for two days.
Mandy	Bonzo is very happy about that.
Mr Wilson	Yes, I think he is, too. Fritz isn't very nice to Bonzo.
Mandy	Can we watch TV now?
Mrs Wilson	Yes, of course.

Scene 5

Later that evening. Mr and Mrs Wilson are watching television in the sitting-room. Peter and Mandy are playing cards on the floor. Mr and Mrs Smith come into the room.

Mrs Smith	Well, I don't know what's the matter with us. But we're really tired. It must be the long car journey today.
Mrs Wilson	I think we all need an early night tonight. Peter and Mandy, time for bed.
Mandy and Peter	Oh no!
Mandy	We just want to finish our game.
Mr Smith	Where are Bonzo and Fritz?
Mr Wilson	I don't know. Isn't Fritz with you?

journey [ˈdʒɜːnɪ] Fahrt
to finish a game [ˈfɪnɪʃ] zu Ende spielen

Mrs Smith	Oh no! I hope they're not in the same room. Bonzo doesn't really like Fritz.
Peter	Fritz doesn't like Bonzo, you mean.
Mrs Smith	Oh dear. We must look for them. Perhaps they're fighting?
Mrs Wilson	Quick, Mandy and Peter, go and look in the garden for Fritz and Bonzo. *(Peter and Mandy run into the kitchen.)*
Mr Smith	Oh dear. I hope Fritz is okay.
Mrs Smith	Yes, me too.
Mandy	*(from the kitchen)* Hey, here they are. They're not in the garden at all. They're both sleeping in Bonzo's basket.

the same [seɪm] der (die, das) Gleiche
to mean [mi:n] meinen
quick [kwɪk] schnell

Mrs Wilson	What! But Bonzo never sleeps in his basket. He always sleeps on Peter's bed.
Mandy	I think they're friends at last. How funny!
Bonzo	*(thinks)* What's so funny? People are funny, not dogs.

1. *Why must Mandy and Peter put on some other clothes?*
2. *What must Mandy and Peter do after breakfast?*
3. *Does Bonzo want to play with the poodle? How do you know?*
4. *What happens at lunch?*
5. *What do the children do in the afternoon?*
6. *What do Mandy and Peter think of Caroline and Nigel?*
7. *"People are funny, not dogs". What do you think?*

Bonzo goes on a picnic

Characters

Bonzo
Mrs Wilson
Peter Wilson
Mike, Peter's friend
Mandy Wilson
Mr Wilson
Mr Park
Jill Park, Mandy's friend
Woman with a green bag
Man with a green bag
Young woman
Boy
Fat man
Woman (and family) with a cat
Mother
Young girl
People on the beach

Scene 1

In the Wilsons' sitting-room. Mandy and Peter are looking for a ball. Mr and Mrs Wilson are packing the food. Bonzo is running around the room.

character ['kærəktə] Charakter, Person
to pack [pæk] packen
to run around the room [ə'raʊnd] im Zimmer umherrennen

Mrs Wilson	So have we got everything? Bonzo, don't run around the room. I'm feeling ill.
Peter	He's so happy.
Mike	Why?
Mandy	Because we're going on a picnic. Bonzo really likes picnics.
Mr Wilson	Mmm, I think so. Cups, lemonade, apples, biscuits ... eh ... sausages ... *(Bonzo goes to Mr Wilson.)*
Mr Wilson	No, Bonzo. The sausages aren't for you.
Mandy	Typical!
Mike	Can't he have a sausage?
Mrs Wilson	Well, he can have *one* sausage. But he usually wants more than one sausage.
Mr Wilson	And we like sausages, too. He often forgets this!
Mrs Wilson	Mandy, where's Jill? What time is she coming?
Mandy	I don't know. 10 o'clock, I think. *(The doorbell rings.)*
Mrs Wilson	Ah that must be her now. *(She goes to the door.)*

sausage ['sɒsɪdʒ] Wurst
typical ['tɪpɪkl] typisch
to ring [rɪŋ] läuten

Mr Wilson	Hello, Mr Park. Hello, Jill. Come in.
Mr Park	It's very nice of you to take Jill on your picnic. You're lucky, it's really nice and sunny today.
Mr Wilson	Yes, we *are* lucky. Perhaps we can swim in the sea. Have you got a swimming costume with you, Jill?
Jill	Yes, and my sunglasses.
Mandy	Oh no! Where are *my* sunglasses?
Bonzo	*(thinks)* Where are *my* sunglasses?
Mrs Wilson	I don't know, Mandy. You can never find anything in Mandy's room.
Mr Park	*(He laughs.)* I know someone like that. Em … What's her name?
Jill	I don't know.
Mr Park	So what time can I fetch Jill?
Mrs Wilson	Oh, you don't need to. We can take her home.
Mr Park	Oh, that's very nice of you. See you later then. Have fun. Bye.
Jill	Bye, Dad.
Mrs Wilson	So have we got everything?

swimming costume [ˈswɪmɪŋ ˌkɒstjuːm] Badeanzug
sunglasses [ˈsʌnglɑːsɪz] Sonnenbrille
anything [ˈenɪθɪŋ] irgendetwas
to need [niːd] brauchen
everything [ˈevrɪθɪŋ] alles

Mr Wilson	Yes, I think so. Food, swimming costumes, a ball. Anything else? *(Bonzo looks up.)* Oh ... eh ... what about Bonzo?
Bonzo	Woof.
Mr Wilson	Do you want to stay at home, Bonzo? Then you can look after the house.
Bonzo	*(thinks)* No, I don't!
Peter	Bonzo is coming with us. A picnic isn't a picnic without Bonzo.
Bonzo	*(thinks)* Just my idea of fun. A picnic, a walk, the sea and a journey in the car. And some nice people, too – my pet Peter, his friend Mike, Mandy and her friend, Jill. Perhaps I can find some cats, too. Then I can run after them. Mmm, I am a happy dog. Just a few of those sausages and it's a wonderful day.

without [wɪˈðaʊt] ohne
journey [ˈdʒɜːnɪ] Fahrt

Scene 2

At Whitby Sands. They walk towards the beach.

Mrs Wilson	Who can see the sea?
Jill	I can. It's very blue today.
Mandy	Yes, but there's a lot of wind.
Mr Wilson	Well, I don't think we're the only people here today. The beach is really full.
Mrs Wilson	Well, Whitby Sands is very popular and on a day like this ...
Mandy	Where can we sit down?
Peter	*(to Mike)* Over there. There's a nice girl with a red hat.
Mike	Where? I can't see a girl with a red hat.
Peter	There.
Mandy	*(to Jill)* Typical!
Mrs Wilson	What about over there? Next to that man and woman with the green bag.
Mr Wilson	Okay. Come on, kids.
Mrs Wilson	*(to the man and woman with the green bag)* Hello. Can we sit here?
Woman	Yes, of course.
Mandy	I'm going for a swim.

popular ['pɒpjʊlə] beliebt
kid [kɪd] umgangssprachliches Wort für Kind
to go for a swim schwimmen gehen

Peter	Me, too.
Jill and Mike	Yes, me, too.
Peter	Are you coming, Bonzo?
Bonzo	*(thinks)* That's a silly question! *(Peter, Mandy, Jill and Mike run to the water. Bonzo runs after them.)*
Peter	*(to Mike)* Let's race the girls to the sea.
Mandy	Come on, Jill. *(They all stand next to the water.)*
Peter	Ooh. It's very cold. *(He puts one foot in the water.)*
Mike	Ooh, yes. Very cold.

to race [reɪs] um die Wette laufen

Mandy You're just a big baby, Peter. *(She gets in the water.)* Come on, Jill. The last person in the water buys all the ice-creams. *(Jill and Mike get into the water after Mandy. Peter is last.)*

Jill Peter is last. Peter is last.

Peter No, I'm not. Bonzo is.

Jill But Bonzo can't buy the ice-creams.

Peter Then we can't have any.

Mandy But that's not fair. You must buy them, Peter.

Jill Where's the ball? Let's play with the ball.

Mike Here, Mandy. *(He throws the ball to her. Peter hits the ball with his hand. It flies through the air.)*

Mandy Oh no! Our ball. Look. Oh there's so much wind. Oh quick. Let's get it.
(Peter, Mandy and Bonzo start to swim after the ball.)

Peter I can't swim any more. I'm tired.

Mandy Me, too.

Peter Let's swim back to the beach.

the last person [lɑ:st], ['pɜ:sn] die letzte Person
ice-cream [ˌaɪs'kri:m] Eiskrem
not … any keine
fair [feə] gerecht
quick [kwɪk] schnell
tired ['taɪəd] müde

Mandy	Oh look. Bonzo is swimming towards the ball. Go on, Bonzo.
Peter	Go on, Bonzo. Good boy.
Mandy	He's got the ball.
Mike	Hooray!
Peter	Clever Bonzo.
	(Bonzo arrives back with the ball.)
Jill	Let's get out of the water now. I'm cold.
Mike	Good idea.
Peter	Who's a clever dog, Bonzo?
	(They all run back to Mr and Mrs Wilson. Bonzo is very happy. He shakes his body. The man and woman with the green bag next to them are very wet.)

to shake [ʃeɪk] (sich) schütteln

Woman	Oh no! I'm all wet. Look.
Man	Me, too. Your dog …
Mrs Wilson	Oh, I'm really sorry. Bonzo! Bad boy.
Mr Wilson	Yes, I'm very sorry. Can we give you some chocolate or some apples?
Man	No! … Thanks.
Mrs Wilson	Oh dear. Now Bonzo. Just sit there and be quiet. No more sea for you! Now who wants a sandwi…
Peter	Bonzo, Bonzo. Come back.
Mandy	Bonzo, Bonzo. Oh no! It's a cat. That family has got a cat. *(Peter and Mandy run after him. Bonzo runs after the cat. He runs over people. He kicks their food. Sandwiches fly through the air. Bottles fall over.)*

Young woman	Hey! You terrible dog. Come back! My sandwiches are in the sand.
Boy	Hey! My lemonade. Oh no! Is that your dog?
Peter	Yes, I'm afraid he's running after that cat ... I'm very sorry ... em ... we can buy you some more lemonade.
Fat man	*(He is eating an ice-cream.)* Oh you terrible dog. Look at my ice-cream. Half of it is in the sand and half of it is on my shirt.
Mandy	Oh, I'm sorry. We can buy you another ice-cream.
Fat man	Where are your mother and father?
Mandy	Over there.
Fat man	I want to speak to them. Terrible dog.
Peter	Bonzo, come here. *(Bonzo stops suddenly and goes to Peter. Mandy picks the cat up and carries it in her arms.)*
Peter	You bad, bad dog. No sausages for you now.
Mandy	That's right. *(Mandy and Peter take the cat back to the family.)*

Bonzo *(thinks)* Why are they all so angry? It's only a silly cat.

Mandy I'm very sorry about Bonzo.

Woman with the cat That's okay. Sometimes these things happen.

(Mandy and Peter walk back to Mr and Mrs Wilson.)

Mr Wilson Bonzo, sit down and stay there. You terrible dog.

Mike Does he often run after cats?

Peter He sometimes runs after Fred, our neighbour's cat.

Mr Wilson Well, who wants a sandwich? No, Bonzo, no sandwich for you.

Bonzo: *(thinks)* What! But I'm hungry, too.

Mrs Wilson Who wants an apple?

Peter and Jill Me, please.

Mandy Can I have another sandwich?

Mr Wilson Yes, here they are.

Mrs Wilson I think I want to sleep a little now.

Mr Wilson Yes, that's a good idea. Can you play over there, kids? Bonzo, you can stay here.

(Peter, Mandy, Mike and Jill play in the sand.)

Mike What can we make?

Jill A castle?

Peter	No, that's silly. I know – a boat.
Mandy	That's silly, too. I know ...
	(Bonzo starts to bark.)
Peter	Stop it Bonzo.
	(Bonzo barks and barks.)
Mandy	Bonzo, stop it.
Mr + Mrs Wilson	Bonzo!
	(Bonzo runs to the sea.)
Mrs Wilson	Oh, Bonzo. Come back.
Mike	What's he doing now?
Mr Wilson	I don't know. Peter, go and get him.
Mandy	Hey, look.
Peter	What?
Mandy	There's a girl in the water. She can't swim. Bonzo is saving her.
Peter	Oh yes, I can see her now.
Jill	Quick, let's go down to the sea.
	(They run to the sea.)
Peter	Go on, Bonzo.
	(Bonzo swims to the beach with the girl on his back. The girl's mother arrives.)
Mother	*(She is crying.)* Oh no, my daughter. Oh.
Peter	It's okay. Bonzo has got her.

to save [seɪv] retten
back [bæk] Rücken

Mother	Oh thank God.
	(The girl is crying. The mother goes into the water and takes her child off Bonzo's back.)
Mother	Oh, Jenny, are you okay? There, there. Don't cry now. Mummy is here.
Jill	Is Jenny okay?
Mother	Yes, she's just afraid. But I think she's okay. Now, what about your dog, Bonzo? What can I give him?
Mandy	He really likes sausages.
Mother	Oh dear, I don't have any sausages. What about ice-creams? Get some ice-creams for everyone and two for Bonzo, of course. Here's some money.
	(Mandy and Jill go and buy the ice-creams.)
Mike	How old is Jenny?
Mother	She's four. Now, where are your parents? I must say thank you to them, too.
Peter	They're just over there.
Mrs Wilson	How is your child now?
Mother	Oh, Jenny is okay.

Thank God. [gɒd] Gott sei Dank.

(Mandy and Jill come back with the ice-creams.)

Mandy Here's your money and here are the ice-creams. One for everyone and two for Bonzo.

Mother Oh thanks.

Mr + Mrs Wilson Thanks very much.

Mr Wilson Well, Bonzo – so perhaps you're not that terrible after all.

Bonzo *(thinks)* Of course I'm not terrible! No sausages, but some ice-creams. How nice. Everyone is happy at last.

1. *Why does Bonzo say, "It's a wonderful day"?*
2. *Why must Peter buy the ice-creams?*
3. *What happens when Bonzo runs after the cat?*
4. *Why does Bonzo run into the sea again?*
5. *Why do they all get ice-creams?*
6. *Do you think Bonzo is terrible? Why? Why not? Say something about him. These words may help you: nice, silly, funny, good friend, likes sausages and walks ...*